EFFECTIVE TEACHING IN THE EARLY YEARS: FOSTERING CHILDREN'S LEARNING IN NURSERIES AND IN INFANT CLASSES

Tricia David, Audrey Curtis,
Iram Siraj-Blatchford

An OMEP (UK) Report

First published in 1992 by Trentham Books Ltd
Reprinted 1996

Trentham Books Limited
Westview House
734 London Road
Oakhill
Stoke-on-Trent
England ST4 5NP

British Cataloguing in Publication Data
A catalogue record for this book is available from the British Library
ISBN: 0 948080 81 7

Acknowledgements
The authors wish to thank Margaret Brown, Mary Doyle, Margaret
Hewitt, Cathy Nutbrown, Kathy Sylva, John Siraj-Blatchford and
Roy David for their help in preparing this document; also, Sandra
Dowse, Margaret Handy and Donna Jay for their hard work and
support with the typing and administration.

Designed and typeset by Trentham Print Design Ltd, Chester and
printed by Bemrose Shafron (Printers) Ltd, Chester.

OMEP

OMEP (Organisation Mondiale pour l'Education Préscolaire — the World Organisation for Early Childhood Education) is an international, non-governmental, multi-agency organisation whose primary aim is to promote, worldwide, the health, education and rights of children aged from birth to eight. OMEP members work regionally, nationally and internationally to:

- promote optimal conditions for the well-being and healthy development of all children;
- assist with projects aimed at improving the life experiences of young children;
- support and publicize research contributing to our understanding of, and work with, children and their families;
- promote developmentally appropriate early childhood education, and education for peace in the world.

Iram Siraj-Blatchford is Lecturer in Early Years Education at the University of London Institute of Education and a member of OMEP; Audrey Curtis is a Senior Lecturer at the University of London Institute of Education and is OMEP's European Vice--President; Tricia David is Professor of Education at Christ Church College, University of Canterbury and she chairs OMEP (UK).

Summary

- Young children's learning experiences are most efficient when they are relevant, meaningful, and active, and are provided in a challenging but familiar context.

- Teachers of young children tend to be pragmatists — they try to find out what 'works' in fostering each child's learning. If dogmas are widespread, they are presumably more likely to be found in 'teacher-directed' classrooms and schools than in 'child-directed', since the latter are extremely rare.

- Research evidence about the superiority of whole class teaching over group and individual work at Key Stage 2 is inconclusive, and research evidence for the early years indicates that more whole class teaching than already occurs would not benefit children in this age group.

- Early years teachers recognise subject divisions in their planning and recording, but offer children relevant, holistic experiences through thematic work, to help them transfer understandings.

- Early years teachers have maintained standards in the basics, while improving standards in the other areas of the National Curriculum. If reading standards have declined, this is now known to be in those areas where children's lives have become more stressful during the last few years.

- Teacher expectations and teachers' levels of training have an effect on children's school experiences, progress and interest in learning. Every other European Community country is moving towards longer teacher education and training, greater synthesis of theory and practice, more course-work on how children develop and learn.

We need a vision for the future to which we can work and which will help us improve children's lives, including their lives in schools. We need a greater commitment to funding the years before five; to education and training for all who work with our youngest children; and we need to ask ourselves whether the education we provide *all* our children is high quality, purposeful and relevant to the lives they lead now, and will have in the 21st Century.

Introduction

Early years practitioners have, for many years, argued that young children benefit from opportunities to learn through first hand experience, individually or in groups, for significant proportions of their school day (eg. Bathurst, 1905; McMillan,1912; Isaacs, 1929) as opposed to being subjected to whole class, teacher-directed approaches. In this document we present research undertaken during the last twenty years which supports their argument. The research has provided qualifying riders which have led us to refine our ideas about children's learning and effective practice in early childhood education.

The publication of reports in which children aged 4 to 11 are seen as a homogeneous group of learners is unhelpful, and the discussion document published recently as the initiator of a debate about good primary practice, *Curriculum Organisation and Classroom Practice in Primary Schools* (Alexander et al, 1992), failed to include some of the evidence available about the early years of schooling. This may have been unintentional on the part of the authors, who may indeed have considered their brief required them to focus on the later years. The discussion document (Alexander et al, 1992) states:

> 'This report reviews available evidence about the delivery of education in primary schools' in order 'to make recommendations about curriculum organisation, teaching methods and classroom practice appropriate for the successful implementation of the National Curriculum particularly in Key Stage 2.' (Par. 1)

However, the document uses some evidence from research conducted in Key Stage 1 classrooms and comments on teaching in Key Stage 1. Further, even if the authors (Alexander et al, 1992) had

7

confined their explorations to Key Stage 2, it would have been naive to assume that any changes emanating from ensuing deliberations would not have had serious repercussions for teachers in Key Stage 1 and nursery classes. Those of us who have, for many years, worked in the early years field know all too well the effects of the practice and expectations in the junior/middle phase upon the earlier stages of education. For this reason we felt it imperative to write an early years 'report', a short, complementary 'sister' guide, to be considered in conjunction with that of the 'three wise men'.

This document by three members of OMEP(UK), all early years specialists, who have had extensive experience of classroom teaching and management in schools (including headships), attempts to highlight areas of importance to early years practitioners, and to address some of the omissions of the official discussion document. Naturally there can be no hope of extensive coverage of the issues, but we suggest that interested colleagues may wish to follow up the research documents cited, to discuss their own interpretations of the evidence, and for this reason they are given in the text. We hope our document will provide early years practitioners, parents, governors, policy makers and politicians with fundamental information on which they may base discussions of practice aimed at improving provision for all the youngest children in our schools.

This report will consider three questions:-

- what do we know about how young children learn?

- what do we know about life in early years classrooms and schools?

- do we have a vision for the future, and how should early years teachers be educated and trained in order that they provide excellent education for all?

What do we know about how young children learn?

No programme of teaching can be successful if we do not take into account the characteristics of young children and how they learn. The nursery and infant school years cover an important period of change and development in children's thinking and in their ability to make sense of the world. Every adult who has worked with this age range knows that the healthy child is active, curious and highly motivated to learn.

But how do they learn? Is their thinking qualitatively different from adults' or is it lack of experience which produces unexpected replies to our questions? For decades the issue of how children learn has exercised the minds of educators, philosophers, sociologists and psychologists. In the first half of this century behaviourist psychologists like Pavlov, Thorndike and Skinner had an important influence upon the ways in which children were taught and there was much emphasis upon rote learning and the need for 'intermittent schedules of reinforcement' — irregular periods of practice.

Gradually it was realised that traditional learning theories, based upon principles of stimulus and response could not account for all aspects of children's learning and educators turned to the ideas of Piaget (1971) and Susan Isaacs, to help them understand how children learn. Piaget saw children's intellectual development as a process of change with the children learning through active interaction with the environment. Piaget argued that a young child's thinking is qualitatively different from the adult's, and Isaacs' detailed observations of children provided powerful insights into the holistic nature of children's learning.

In recent years there has been criticism of Piaget's views that children's understanding depends upon their stage of development. Donaldson (1978) suggests that young children's inability to carry out correctly some of the Piagetian tasks was due to their failure to understand what was required of them. She argued that all learning takes place within a particular context and if the child's expectations, based upon previous knowledge of the world, are different from the teacher's expectations then the child will 'fail'. This, in her view, results from a communication problem between adult and child. In order to help the child move from a context bound situation to disembedded thinking we need to view the situation from the child's point of view.

Researchers like McGarrigle and Donaldson (1974), Gelman (1969) and Bryant and Trabasso (1971) have demonstrated that young children can understand problems at an earlier stage than Piaget had suggested *if* they appreciate what is required from them.

Action and problem solving are of importance in the learning process as indicated by much research including Wood, Bruner and Ross (1976), and Sylva (1976), who argued that concrete experience is crucial in helping children towards abstract thinking. Their research, and that of many others, has demonstrated that children do not learn as successfully if they are simply told or shown what to do rather than given the opportunity to experiment for themselves. As Donaldson and her colleagues commented, learning will be inefficient if it lacks meaning for the child.

· Language has a fundamental role to play in the development of learning and understanding. For Bruner (1983) and Vygotsky (1978), language, communication and instruction are at the heart of intellectual and personal development. In talking the adult acts as facilitator, providing the 'scaffolding' which enables the child to make sense of her world. The child who cannot solve a problem or memorize an experience on her own, may well be able to do so with the help of an adult.

Whereas Bruner speaks of the adult as providing the scaffolding, Vygotsky talks of the 'zone of proximal development', that is the gap between what the child is able to do alone and what she can attain with the help of someone more knowledgeable than herself. It is through language and social interaction that adults transmit the knowledge and values of their culture to children. This transmission of societal and cultural values is normally through adults, although there are examples in the literature where other children can provide the appropriate 'scaffolding' (Azimita, 1988).

Learning from each other / collaborative learning

Vygotsky argued that 'cooperatively achieved success' is fundamental to learning. The instruction which the more knowledgeable person gives to another with lesser skills enables learning to take place. Azimita's research (1988) has shown that sometimes it is other children who transmit the necessary knowledge. Furthermore it has been found that when children collaborate on a problem solving task, they are more likely to reach a solution than if they tried to solve the problem alone (Forman and Cazden, 1985). Communication within a group, even where there are differing and incorrect opinions will produce positive learning effects (Doise and Mugny, 1984).

Cooperative learning takes place effectively in many play situations. By playing together and trying out new ideas and combinations of skills, children are able to come to understand many of the skills and behaviours that are expected of them by the adult world. Bruner has argued that it is in the play situation that young children can come to test their ideas and knowledge in innovative combinations, independently from the adults whose role has been that of structuring the play opportunities. Sylva et al (1980) stressed the value of children working in pairs and pointed out that higher levels of complexity in play and language were to be found in these situations.

Although learning is an interactive process, best facilitated by the appropriate intervention of adults, there are other factors which need to be considered which may affect children's learning. Motivation is one important factor. Activities which stem from the child's interests and therefore produce intrinsic motivation are more likely to lead to effective learning. This is one of the reasons why rigid instruction programmes like the Bereiter and Englemann (1966) were less successful with Headstart children in the USA than the guided play situations advocated by the High/Scope programme (Weikart et al, 1971), a curriculum which is structured by highly trained professionals.

Other relevant factors include memory and recall and concentration. Piaget argued that the child's ability to memorise material is a function of age, and there is no doubt that young children have difficulties in recalling information accurately. However it seems that children have most difficulty in concentrating and recalling when the task does not match their understanding. The 'problem of the match' is one of the most difficult challenges for the educator. Children in this age group (ie. 3-7) are very unlikely to have developed mental strategies like rehearsal, or to be able to organise their thoughts about what they already know, recalling their knowledge in a meaningful way in order to use it for new learning experiences. For this reason the adult acting as facilitator will be, among other things, 'memory bank', 'prompt', 'sounding board', and 'supporter'.

No psychologist would pretend to be able to give a complete answer to the question 'How do children learn?' but there is sufficient evidence to show that learning is most effective when children are *actively* involved and not passive recipients of information. Adults have a vital role to play in transmitting the knowledge and values of different cultures and can best do this by providing the necessary 'scaffolding' in a context which is familiar and meaningful, but challenging.

What do we know about life in early years classrooms?

The possibility of presenting all the research evidence which exists is far too complex for us to do justice to in this brief report. However, we will attempt to present some of the main findings of relevance to the current debate.

The prevalence of dogma

Poor quality of teaching in some schools seems unlikely to be associated with any particular educational 'doctrine' or 'dogma'. We would concur with HMI findings that there is indeed a wide variation in standards in similar schools and similar classes and that this presents a problem that deserves our undivided attention. However we also believe that these variations may be as relevant to didactically taught, subject-based classes as to so called, 'child-centred' classrooms. Since research shows (DES, 1978; Tizard et al, 1988; Desforges and Cockburn, 1987; Bennett and Kell, 1989) that 'progressive' teaching methods are a great rarity, they can hardly be blamed for alleged low standards within the system as a whole.

Child-centred practice

The view that child-centred educators fail to provide any encounter between pupils' 'personal understandings and the public knowledge embodied in our cultural traditions' (Alexander et al, 1992; par.64) begs the question of whose cultural traditions are being referred to and, more importantly, misrepresents child centred practice.

Where the curriculum has been based on first-hand experience, the teacher structures certain activities so that children may explore and experiment (see for example the HMI publications DES, 1987, 1989a,b,c,d, 1990a, 1990b). Then, teachers, acting as facilitators, build on that relevant experience and offer a further range of experiences, depending on their assessment of the child's learning needs. This may range from direct, didactic teaching, to the encouragement to represent, interpret, evaluate, and transform, or be creative with, ideas about those experiences. We have evidence about the experience and development of the role of teacher as 'facilitator', or 'mediator', which is based on Vygotsky's work (1978) from, for example, Wood et al (1980), Desforges and Cockburn (1987). These studies indicate the crucial and varied nature of adult intervention in learning.

The idea that children are never told or taught may stem from research in classrooms where teachers were unsure of what was required of them (Campbell and David, 1989; Alexander, 1992). For experienced child-centred practitioners meaningful questioning, explaining and 'telling' are widely recognised as consistent and essential techniques to be adopted in the process of learning.

Children may label some school activities as 'play'. Indeed, play with or without an adult's participation, may form part of the pattern of a child's day in the early years, but research has shown that even in reception classes deemed to offer 'good practice' by three local authorities, 4 year-old children actually played for only 8 per cent of their day (Bennett and Kell, 1989). Much longer periods of the day are commonly spent in play (28%) at breaks and 'dinnertime' by children in all age-groups (Blatchford, 1989). In other words, it would appear that, if there has indeed been a decline in standards, it cannot be attributed to 'play methods' or 'child-directed' classrooms — they have never really been tried in sufficient numbers to so affect the nation's educational standards.

In fact, HMI (DES, 1991) surveys indicate that standards in Key Stage 1 have been generally better than Key Stage 2 over the past two years so presumably this would suggest that 'child-centred' practices, which are more widely applied in infant classrooms and more readily taught on early years specialist courses in teacher training, are more effective, and indeed, such methods have been endorsed by the Government-convened 'Rumbold Committee' (DES, 1990a).

Wasting children's time

Research about children starting school (eg. see Willes, 1983; Stevenson, 1987) has demonstrated just how much valuable learning time is wasted in the first year in school, through inappropriate, too formal teaching methods. Many primary schools have worked hard to improve this situation for the youngest children in reception classes, but care needs to be taken in any discussion of moves to more whole class, or specialist teaching, that very young children's needs, and 'fitness for purpose', are not overlooked in the moves to change practice in classes for older children. Less of children's time would be wasted if there were better adult:child ratios in early years classrooms.

Organisation

a) 'Fitness for purpose'

It is important for teachers to use a variety of teaching styles, ranging from whole class, to group, to individual, using the notion devised by Mortimore (1992) of 'fitness for purpose', and this is endorsed by Alexander et al (1992). It is the act of making decisions about which children and which subjects or topics should be taught using which style which make teaching young children a very complex task. Thus, 'fitness for purpose' in relation to teaching very young children must take account of the active nature of the learning process, as discussed above.

b) Individualisation and match

Alexander et al (1992) argue that we need to match the task with the pupil and yet at the same time *substantially* increase whole class teaching to the detriment of providing children with the extra support in small groups under the kind of close supervision they need for some tasks. They argue that appropriate differentiation is 'hopelessly unrealistic' and that our classroom organisation and teaching methods should not be grounded upon those principles(110). While at the same time they argue: 'effective assessment and record keeping are more likely to occur in schools which recognise that pupils' progress depends upon assessing their strengths and weaknesses.'(113) Surely the whole purpose of assessment and record keeping is to facilitate the provision of appropriately differentiated curricula, and differentiation now a legal requirement (DES, 1989d)?

Teachers of young children have found it necessary to focus, as the Plowden Report (CACE, 1967) urged, on individual children and their learning needs ('at the heart of the education process lies the child'). The matching of the curriculum to the child is central to good practice, it is as useless to present children with tasks which are too easy, as it is to present them with tasks which are too difficult. Trying to match the work in an exact way is indeed very difficult (Bennett et al, 1984), but it is well-nigh impossible if the teacher does not know the children's individual strengths and weaknesses, and if the teacher does not understand the ways in which developmental psychology can inform practice. This view is supported by the British Psychological Society's (BPS, 1992) Media Release on 'Teaching Styles in the Primary Classroom'.

Daniel Stern (1977) used a beautiful analogy when explaining how some parents are more effective than others in fostering their babies' development, although the effect is similar to that achieved by the behaviour delineated in the analogy of 'scaffolding', it is the analogy of 'the dance'. Parents who learn to adjust their 'dance' to their child's , who try to make sense of their baby's attempts at early communication and interaction will bring that baby on much faster than those who expect their baby to adjust to them. Perhaps this sensitivity to the 'dance' is the secret of good practice in teaching, whatever the age of the learner. What we do know, however, is that this type of practice is very demanding in classrooms with one adult to a large number of young children (Desforges and Cockburn, 1987), but we also know that certain types of classroom organisation, where children are given time to work on self-chosen tasks, and where there is skilled and careful planning of resources and classroom procedures, teachers are freed to spend more time with individual children. Further, that the children will often select tasks that offer the most appropriate challenge, or 'match' for them (Sylva et al, 1980; Campbell and David, 1990).

Other studies show how hard committed infant teachers will work to try to offer children appropriate, first-hand experience but that their failures have more to do with the impossible nature of the task of teaching small children without adequate staffing ratios (Desforges and Cockburn, 1987), and HMI (DES, 1991) reiterate the need for skilled classroom help from nursery nurses and ancillaries.

c) Whole class teaching

The authors of the official discussion document call for more whole class teaching, but also for discrimination as to when such teaching would be appropriate. We argue that early years teachers already make such decisions for a variety of practical reasons, such as, small group teaching in much of the work involved in the Science Programmes of Study. Here, it is not only the children's learning needs which are taken into account, but also resourcing and children's safety.

Greater proportions of time spent on whole class teaching is not the answer for our youngest children, for the reasons cited in different sections, above. The criticism of *working on too many different activities or subjects simultaneously* (97) may have more to do with the lack of adequate planning and rigour in practice, than in this style of working. This type of organisation was formerly labelled 'progressive' or 'informal', but as the BPS (1992) point out, there is no research evidence to indicate the efficacy of 'formal' over 'progressive' methods. Bennett's (1976) study is often quoted in support of this argument, yet the teacher whose children outperformed all others was 'informal' in the classroom. What was important here was that this teacher was 'formal' in the sense that she planned, assessed, recorded and evaluated most conscientiously. Further, consideration must be given to evidence from the USA

(Katz, 1987; Zigler, 1987) warning of young children 'burning out' as a result of too early formalisation. Further, some of our European partners who have been cited as paragons of 'formality' and whole class teaching are moving away from this style of work with young children (Fargeas, 1992).

One wonders if any of the LEAs where reading standards at 7 are said to have declined are those where children began to be taken into formal reception classes at 4 years old, without any appropriate alterations to resourcing and practice.

Examples of research evidence indicating the importance of varied organisational approaches include the following: Sylva and her colleagues' study (1980) demonstrated how certain activities offered cognitive challenge in a way that others did not, and part of that challenge lay in the children's experiences working in pairs, directing their own learning; Meadows' work with Cashdan (1988) provided other evidence about ways to offer such challenge, and their report indicates the extent to which we may be underestimating the intellectual capabilities of young children.

It is possible that teachers are most adept in the use of a variety of teaching styles, including groupwork, when they feel most confident in their own levels of subject knowledge (Alexander, 1988) and when they have undertaken courses which have specifically focused on groupwork, for example (Doyle, 1986).

d) Cross curricular work (topic) and/or subjects
In the discussion document there are some confusing statements about early years teachers, for example, in par. 65 *'teachers (often of younger pupils) ...prefer to view the curriculum in terms of broad areas'*. Firstly, this does not mean they are incapable of planning and evaluating work in terms of subjects.

Secondly, Alexander et al (1992) argue that subject disciplines represent: *'the most powerful tools for making sense of the world which human beings have ever devised'* (64). Not only do we believe that concept formation is generally facilitated by approaches from a number of perspectives, we are also conscious of a body of informed opinion that argues that increasingly professional subject specialisation has led to a dangerous lack of economic adaptability in a rapidly changing world. We are also aware of the lack of concern that has often been shown by specialist scientists and technologists for the by-products of short term developments in terms of pollution and standards of living.

HMI (DES, 1989a), in the very document used to suggest that topic work leads to weak teaching in history and geography, argue that 'Topic work was an important and integral part of the curriculum in all the schools where there was good practice' (DES, 1989a; par.46). Additionally, in commenting on the implementation of the National Curriculum at Key Stage 1, HMI (DES, 1991) state that 'there was some good cross-curricular work in topics' (par.1) and that topic work has 'generally improved...more schools were attempting to secure continuity across year groups by discussing topic frameworks which cover a Key Stage or the whole school.' (Par.28)

As far as the National Curriculum is concerned, the non-statutory guidance for all of the subjects so far introduced stresses the value of subject integration. We are not contesting the value of subject based curriculum planning, assessment or recording but we feel that if themes are to be introduced through subjects then some subjects may well, in our opinion, neglect important themes. For example, Home Economics provides early years teachers with many varied activities. These are not only relevant and meaningful to young children, but they also offer learning experiences within which teachers can identify subject-specific elements.

Key Stage 1 teachers apply the National Curriculum, discriminating between the subjects. A great deal of on-going effort is being made to study them in order to integrate them rationally and Key Stage 1 teachers have been warmly congratulated by HMI (DES, 1991) for their considerable efforts. Their conscientiousness in this task, in working to present the Programmes of Study in ways which will be meaningful to young children, has been reported (Campbell et al, 1991).

Standards

The alleged fall in reading standards indicated by NFER (Gorman and Fernandes, 1992) research in the period 1987-91 may well have been due to the disruption caused by the intemperate pace of introduction in National Curriculum and Assessment procedures during the same period. Alexander et al (1992) suggest that the alleged deterioration in numeracy is due to the lack of *'teachers' knowledge, skills and understanding in the subject'* (72) and that *'to function effectively in the 21st century, our children will need higher standards of literacy and numeracy than ever before'* (25). However, they also comment that *'Pupils are more likely — to spend a higher proportion of time off task in the reading and writing tasks which dominate mathematics and English than when engaged in other activities'* (76ii).

The evidence cited concerning teachers' own expertise in mathematics is somewhat confusing. We are told that children's performance in 'geometry', 'measures', 'probability' and 'statistics' have improved, yet these are far more 'specialised' areas of mathematics than the basic number categories, which included 'decimals' and 'fractions' that we are told have seen a deterioration. In fact this whole argument is contradicted directly by the admitted improvements made in science and technology, including information technology by non-specialist teachers. Further, concentrating again on 'the basics', the most recent evidence from NFER (Gorman and Fernandes, 1992) on reading standards, indicates that there has not been a general decline, but that children living in poverty are those most likely to be under-achieving, presumably as a result of their stressful and impoverished lives.

Evidence about 'the basics' from research by Tizard et al (1988) indicates that this is often the kind of work children find uninteresting. 'Although most children enjoyed school, less than half found their lessons interesting' (Tizard et al, 1988; p.185), and children complained that they found reading and spelling particularly frustrating. Interestingly, these researchers suggest that the remedy lies in 'the new 'developmental' primary teaching approaches' which 'may prevent some of these frustrations.'(p.185) We agree that children are less motivated in these 'basics' if they are taught as such, and would like to see publishers taking more interest in progressive integrated packages that support simultaneous attention being given to subject materials, literacy and numeracy.

Further useful evidence about children's oral and written language, and their ability to work independently, comes from the materials generated by the National Oracy Project and the National Writing Project, and from HMI endorsements of these results (DES, 1990b). The higher standards that we should and are aiming for are surely not only in terms of the so called 'basic skills' but much more in terms of developing capability in problem solving and the integration and synthesis of information.

Teacher expectations — Happiness and challenge

Parents in the study by Hughes and his colleagues (1991) reiterated the desire heard by most early years practitioners, that first and foremost they want their children to be happy at this stage in their education. Nancy Elliott, Senior Inspector for Primary Education in Newcastle-upon-Tyne stated, at the 1989 Primary Conference in Scarborough, that some schools are indeed happy places, but damningly, that they can be 'the next best thing to a lobotomy', lacking challenge, and having low expectations of children. If we believe schools should be happy welcoming places we need to explore the ways in which daring to learn, daring to make mistakes, learning to learn and to think, learning to be literate and numerate, to develop the physical, social, emotional, aesthetic, creative, technological, scientific, spiritual and moral aspects of our humanity, can be universally available and at the same time exhilaratingly enjoyable.

It is undeniable that teacher expectations need to be raised in some particularly inner city schools. There is a growing body of research that demonstrates this (see for example, Tizard et al, 1988; Ross and Tomlinson, 1991). However it also needs to be recognised that standards have often been affected by a vicious cycle of educational failure, in both schools and communities.

Effects of earlier experience

Some children embarking on their primary school careers in reception class may be judged less of a 'pleasure to teach' than those who adapt quickly to the demands of school (Tizard et al, 1988) and this has been shown to relate to children's earlier experiences. Reduced teacher expectations may be the result. A number of studies raise different aspects of this issue (eg. Barrett, 1986; Crocker and Cheeseman, 1988; Hutt et al, 1989; Jowett and Sylva, 1986). Whatever the cause, research evidence (eg. Knight, forthcoming) is indicating that nursery education has a beneficial effect on later SAT scores, and many children are currently denied access to that foundation. A long and rigorous study by Chris Athey (1990) has demonstrated the tenets of Bronfenbrenner's (1979) theory about the beneficial effects of the empowerment of the parent-child 'dyad', for in her study parents and staff worked very closely together and the nursery education offered was made relevant, ('fit for the purpose'), by the use of careful observation and recording, and by detailed knowledge of each child's learning styles. Further, two House of Commons Select Committees (HoC, 1989, 1991) have recently endorsed the value of nursery education, one, reporting on standards of reading, stressed that the members of the Committee were 'in no doubt of the value of nursery education' (p.xii).

Is the National Curriculum too big, and was the pre-ERA curriculum too small? Should the National Curriculum be made 'just right'?

We have to accept that the possible responses to this general recognition must include:

1. The abandonment of the National Curriculum as currently envisaged and structured or;

2. The adoption and elaboration of setting and streaming practices and the further reintroduction of differential schooling, or;

3. The adoption of more child-centred and progressive methods throughout education and perhaps especially in Key Stage 4 where the greatest diversity will be apparent.

The first option would involve our turning our backs on some major advances that have been made to implement the National Curriculum so far and would probably have a catastrophic effect on teacher morale. The second option would lead to even greater variations in local and national standards and represent a huge step backwards both historically and socially. We therefore favour the last option and believe that it is consistent with many school development plans. Schools have taken the N.C.C. at its word that they would be told *what to* teach and not *how* to teach.

Conclusion — vision for the future

The education system

Alexander, Rose and Woodhead (1992; par 15) touch on the fact that the class teacher system was devised to be 'cheap but efficient'. Desforges and Cockburn (1987) argue that a system which is analogous to a 'Ford', even if 'sooped up', can never become a Rolls Royce. To ensure continuity of experience and, at the same time, sufficient expert support for teachers in subjects other than 'their own' may mean that 'in real terms' pupil:teacher ratios must be altered for the better. This would mean that children would work with people who are familiar to them yet who team teach throughout the school. It seems likely that early years teachers are more used to working in this more flexible way, alongside other colleagues.

Teacher education and training

To argue that 'teaching is not applied child development' (52) and for greater emphasis to be placed on the study of classroom practice (Alexander et al, 1992), is to hint at a real problem for the recent history of enquiry into education. Unfortunately the argument suggests some dichotomy in these approaches, whereas we believe that it is essential to recognise that the study and elaboration of classroom practice and the psychological and socio-psychological study of child development are consistent and complementary activities, not alternative perspectives. These areas of study provide essential understandings upon which to ground rational educational developments. Research (Pascal et al, 1991) is demonstrating that we in the UK will be alone in Europe if we move away from teacher education which is grounded in understandings about how children learn *and* how children develop (surely the two are inseparable?).

We feel that the existing entry qualifications for teacher education courses provide a quite proper and adequate basis for the core areas and that initial teacher training should actually provide a more demanding grounding in all of the National Curriculum subjects and cross curricular elements. In the short term we must recognise that the improvements in science and technology have been achieved through the provision of adequate quality inservice training and if we are concerned for the future what we need to be asking is 'Where are the courses, the supply cover and the commitment to Key Stage 2 and the other subjects?'

While the demands of Key Stage 2 may well cause difficulties for many primary teachers, we certainly do not accept that Key Stage 1 demands create any serious problems for infant teachers. If primary teachers need greater subject knowledge then this suggests the need for continued in-service training. The successful implementation of science and information technology in Key Stage 1 has, so far, demanded and been realised through a substantial commitment to supply cover and to the provision of quality inservice training by local education authorities. We have yet to see if this will be continued throughout the Key Stages and for different subjects. If it is not then we shall not be seeing any failure on the part of teachers, only on the part of Government taking on an over-ambitious project with too tight a schedule and inadequate resourcing to see it through. Furthermore, in-service training and education must offer teachers more than instruction and induction in National Curriculum subjects and assessments. It must give teachers time to share in discussion of the issues and dilemmas involved in practice.

Parents

Increasingly, the part parents play, in educating as well as caring for their young children, is being acknowledged and underpinned by research (eg. Hannon et al, 1991; Tizard and Hughes, 1984). Athey (1990) has shown that parents who, through partnership with professionals, acquire pedagogical knowledge, are able effectively to support and extend children's learning. Teachers in the early years recognise the crucial role of parents, but need time to work with them, developing skills, strategies and confidence to share their own professionalism.

Children's lives

Although it is impossible for us to tell what the lives of these young children will be like in the 21st Century, we need to ask ourselves whether the education being offered is purposeful, and whether it is capable of equipping them *all* to live in a post-industrial, 'high-tech' world, where environmental, health, and other global concerns are likely to become more acute as the years progress.

Our membership of the European Community too may influence our children in ways we have not foreseen.

We have commented upon the effects of poverty on children's attainments. According to some of the most recent evidence (Bradshaw, 1990) this is having profound effects on many children's lives. While home circumstances should never be permitted to be used as excuses for failing to motivate and challenge children, or for low expectations, it must be remembered that parents of young children are more likely to turn to teachers for support if the school ethos is one of caring for them as individuals, and for having time to care about personal development. Most adults recall with affection those teachers they would describe as 'good practitioners', and they will normally add that such a teacher 'knew them, knew what standard of work they wanted of each child, and knew what they were teaching.' In other words, we remember as 'effective practitioners' those teachers who not only knew their subject/s but treated us as individual, interesting, people, who mattered.

We will only improve standards when we have devised and implemented a vision of life-long, high quality education for all.

References

Alexander, R. (1988) 'Garden or jungle?' in A. Blyth (Ed) *Informal Primary Education Today* London, Falmer

Alexander, R. (1992) *Policy and Practice in Primary Education* London, Routledge

Alexander, R., Rose, J. and Woodhead, C. (1992) *Curriculum Organisation and Classroom Practice in Primary Schools* London, HMSO

Athey, C. (1990) *Extending Thought in Young Children* London, PCP

Azmitia, M. (1988) Peer Interaction and Problem Solving: 'When are two better than one?' *Child Development* Vol.59, 1, p.87-96

Barrett, G. (1986) *Starting School: an evaluation of the experience* London, AMMA

Bathurst, K. (1905) 'Report of women inspectors on children under five years of age in elementary schools' reproduced in W.Van der Eyken (Ed) (1975) *Education, the child and society* Harmondsworth, Penguin

Bennett, S.N. (1976) *Teaching styles and pupil progress* London, Open Books

Bennett, N., Desforges, C., Cockburn, A. and Wilkinson, B. (1984) *The Quality of Pupil Learning Experiences* London, LEA

Bennett, N. and Kell, J. (1989) *A Good Start?* Oxford, Blackwell

Bereiter, C. and Englemann, S. (1966) *Teaching Disadvantaged Children* New Jersey, Prentice Hall

Blatchford, P. (1989) *Playtime in the Primary School* Windsor, NFER/Nelson

BPS (1992) *Media Release: Teaching Styles in the Primary School* Leicester, British Psychological Society

Bradshaw, J. (1990) *Child Poverty and Deprivation in the UK* London, National Children's Bureau

Bronfenbrenner, U. (1979) *The Ecology of Human Development* Cambridge MA, Harvard UP

Bruner, J. (1983) *Child's Talk* New York, Norton

Bruner, J. (1966) *Towards a Theory of Instruction* Cambridge MA, Harvard University Press

Bryant, P. and Trabasso, T. (1971) 'Transitive inference and memory in young children' *Nature* 232. p. 456-8

CACE (1967) *Children and their Primary Schools* London, HMSO

Campbell, R.J. and David, T. (1989) *Interim Report: Learning through the school and the local environment* Coventry, University of Warwick

Campbell, R.J. and David, T. (1990) *Depth and Quality in Children's Learning* Coventry, University of Warwick

Campbell, R.J. and Neill, S. St.J. (1990) *Thirteen Hundred and Thirty Days: Final Report of a pilot study of Teacher Time in Key Stage 1 Commissioned by the Assistant Masters and Mistresses Association* Coventry, University of Warwick

Crocker, A.C. and Cheeseman, R.G. (1988) 'Infant teachers have a major impact on children's self-awareness' *Children and Society* 2, 1, p.3-8

DES (1978) *Primary Education in England: a survey by HM Inspectors of Schools* London, HMSO

DES (1987) *Primary Schools: some aspects of good practice* London, HMSO

DES (1989a) *The Teaching and Learning of History and Geography* London, HMSO

DES (1989b) *The Education of Children under Five* London, HMSO

DES (1989c) *The Teaching and Learning of Science* London, HMSO

DES (1989d) *The Teaching and Learning of Mathematics* London, HMSO

DES (1990a) *Starting with Quality* (Rumbold Report) London, HMSO

DES (1990b) *The Teaching and Learning of Language and Literacy* London, HMSO

DES (1991) *The Implementation of the Curricular Requirements of ERA: an Overview by HM Inspectorate on the First Year, 1989-90* London, HMSO

Desforges, C. and Cockburn, A. (1987) *Understanding the Mathematics Teacher* London, Falmer

Doise, W. and Mugny, G. (1984) *The social development of the intellect* Oxford, Pergamon Press

Donaldson, M. (1978) *Children's Minds* Glasgow, Fontana

Doyle, M.F. (1986) 'An exploratory study of the reasons given by teachers for the use of group-work with the age-range 9-11' Unpublished thesis, MA in Education, London University Institute

Fargeas, J. (1992) 'France: nos interrogations les plus pressantes' *European Report* 1,1, p.5-8

Forman, E. and Cazden, C. (1985) 'Exploring Vygotskian perspectives in education: the cognitive value of peer interaction' in Wertsch J.V. (Ed) *Culture, Communication and Cognition: Vygotskian Perspectives* New York, Cambridge University Press

Gelman, R. (1969) 'Conservation Acquisition' *Journal of Experimental Psychology* 7, p.167-87

Gorman, T. and Fernandes, C. (1992) *Reading in Recession* Slough, NFER

Hannon, P., Weinberger, J. and Nutbrown, C. (1991) 'A study of work with parents to promote early literacy development'*Research Papers in Education*, 6, 2, p.77-99

HoC (1989) *Educational Provision for the Under Fives* London, HMSO

HoC (1991) *Standards of Reading in Primary Schools* London, HMSO

Hughes, M., Wikeley, F. and Nash, T. (1991) *Parents and SATs: a second interim report* Exeter, Exeter University School of Education

Hutt, S.J., Tyler, S., Hutt, C. and Christopherson, H. (1989) *Play, Exploration and Learning* London, Routledge

Isaacs, S. (1929) *The Nursery Years* London, RKP

Jowett, S. and Sylva, K. (1986) 'Does kind of pre-school matter?' *Educational Research* 28, 1, p.31-40

Katz, L. (1987) 'Burnout by five' reported in *Times Educational Supplement* 18.9.87

Knight, C. (forthcoming) Work in progress for M.Phil. University of Warwick

McGarrigle, J. and Donaldson, M. (1974) 'Conservation Accidents' *Cognition* 3, p.341-50

McMillan, M. (1912) ''The needs of little children' *Papers for the Women's Labour League*

Meadows, S. and Cashdan, A. (1988) *Helping Children Learn* London, David Fulton

Mortimore, P. (1992) 'Trends in Education and Society in the 1990s' Paper to the Institute of Education Society, London University Institute of Education, 16 March 1992

Pascal, C., Bertram, T. and Heaslip, P. (1991) *Comparative Directory of Initial Training for Early Years Teachers* Worcester, Worcester College

Piaget, J. (1971) *Science of Education and the Psychology of the Child* London, Longmans

Piaget, J. and Inhelder, B. (1969) *The Psychology of the child* London, Routledge and Kegan Paul

Ross, A. and Tomlinson, S. (1991) *Teachers and Parents* London, IPPR

Stern, D. (1977) *The First Relationship: Infant and Mother* London, Fontana/Open Books

Stevenson, C. (1987) 'The young four-year-old in nursery and infant classes: challenges and constraints' in NFER/SCDC Seminar Report *Four year olds in School* London SCDC/NFER

Sylva, K. (1976) 'Problem Solving in young children' in Bruner, J., Jolly, A. and Sylva, K. *Play: its role in development and Evolution* Harmondsworth, Penguin.

Sylva, K., Roy, C. and Painter, M. (1980) *Child Watching at play group and nursery* school London, Grant McIntyre

Tizard, B. and Hughes, M. (1984) *Young Children Learning* London, Fontana

Tizard, B., Blatchford, P.,Burke, J. Farquhar, C. and Plewis, I. (1988) *Young Children in the Inner City* London, LEA

Weikart, D.Rogers,L., Adcock, C. and Mclelland,D. (1971) *The Cognitively Oriented Curriculum* Unbana USA, ERI

Willes, M. (1983) *Children into Pupils* London, RKP

Wood, D. (1988) *How children think and learn* Oxford, Blackwell

Wood, D., Bruner, J. and Ross, G. (1976) 'The role of tutoring in problem-solving' *Journal of Child Psychology and Psychiatry* 17, 2, p.89-100

Wood, D., McMahon, L. and Cranstoun, Y. (1980) *Working with Under Fives* London, Grant McIntyre

Vygotsky, L. (1978) *Mind in Society* Cambridge MA, Harvard.

Vygotsky, L. (1962) *Thought and Language* Cambridge MA, MIT

Zigler, E.F. (1987) 'Formal schooling for four-year-olds? No.' *American Psychologist* 42, 3, p.254-60

INTERNATIONAL JOURNAL OF EARLY CHILDHOOD
Published with the aid of UNESCO Subvention
ISSN 0020-7187

This journal is produced twice each year in June and November. Each issue contains a selection of research papers, practical projects, reports of conferences and news from UNESCO, UNICEF and OMEP.

It includes articles and reports from all the continents, which will reflect the work of OMEP, as well as provide a vehicle for the exchange of work being undertaken in many fields, by those serving young children and their families.

Cost of the Journal is £6 per annum to members of OMEP, £10 to non-members. This includes surface rate mail world-wide (air mail £3 per issue extra). Payment is in £ Sterling and cheques should be made payable to OMEP UK, International Journal Account. Drafts can be paid direct to our Bankers: Midland Bank PLC., The Square, Bakewell, Derbyshire. Bank sort code 40 09 30. Account number 31063685.

Further details about the Journal can be obtained from:

The Editor, Mrs A. Curtis, DCDPE, Institute of Education, University of London, 20 Bedford Way, London WC1A 0AL, UK or,

The Business Manager, M. C. Hewitt, Huntcliffe, Over Lane, Baslow, Bakewell, Derbyshire, DE45 1RT, UK.

ORDER FORM

Please supply/order for me................ copies of OMEP International Journal of Early Childhood @ £6 (member) / £10 (non-member) rate. (delete as required).
I enclose £........................... (words) £............. for a one year subscription.

Please dispatch to: Name...
Address...
....
....Post code............................

Signed.. Date.....................................
I am a member of OMEP... (Country)
My agent is..(Delete as appropriate)
Please return to: **M. C. Hewitt, Huntcliffe, Over Lane, Baslow, Bakewell, Derbyshire DE45 1RT.**
Please pass your order to your agent if desired.